Desert
Animals

by **Sharon Gordon**

Reading Consultant: Nanci R. Vargus, Ed.D.

Marshall Cavendish
Benchmark
New York

Picture Words

 bat

 bobcat

 coyote

 hawk

jackrabbit

 lizard

 rattlesnake

 sun

Many desert animals stay out of the hot .

The rests in the shade.

The hops to a bush.

The flies to a cave.

The lies under a rock.

The  flies to a tree.

The rests in a hole.

The  lies by a bush.

I stay cool from the hot , too.

Words to Know

animals (AN-uh-mahls)
    living things that can move

bush   a plant that grows near
    the ground

cave   an opening in a hill

desert (DEZ-ert)
    a hot, dry place

Find Out More

Books

De Lambilly-Bresson, Elisabeth. *Animals in the Desert*.
Strongsville, OH: Gareth Stevens Publishing, 2007.
Townsend, Emily Rose. *Lizards*. Mankato, MN: Capstone
Press, 2006.
———. *Rattlesnakes*. Mankato, MN: Capstone Press,
2006.

Video

How Desert Creatures Survive. Produced by KUAT-TV in
cooperation with the Arizona-Sonora Desert Museum
and The Nature Conservancy, Arizona Chapter. Tucson:
KUAT-TV.

Web Sites

Blue Planet Biomes: Desert
www.blueplanetbiomes.org/desert.htm
Desert USA: Desert Animals and Wildlife
www.desertusa.com/animal.html
The Living Desert
www.livingdesert.org

About the Author

Sharon Gordon is an author, editor, and advertising copywriter. She is a graduate of Montclair State University in New Jersey and has written more than one hundred children's books, many for Marshall Cavendish, that include works of fiction, nonfiction, and cultural history. Along with her family, she enjoys exploring the plant and animal life of the Outer Banks of North Carolina.

About the Reading Consultant

Nanci R. Vargus, Ed.D., wants all children to enjoy reading. She used to teach first grade. Now she works at the University of Indianapolis. Nanci helps young people become teachers. She used to live near the Mojave Desert in Southern California.

Marshall Cavendish Benchmark
99 White Plains Road
Tarrytown, NY 10591-5502
www.marshallcavendish.us

All Internet addresses were correct at the time of printing.

Library of Congress Cataloging-in-Publication Data
Gordon, Sharon.
Desert animals / by Sharon Gordon.
      p. cm. — (Benchmark Rebus : Animals in the wild)
Summary: "Easy to read text with rebuses explores animals that live in the desert"—Provided by publisher.
Includes bibliographical references.
ISBN 978-0-7614-2898-5
Desert animals—Juvenile literature. I. Title.
QL116.G67 2008
591.754—dc22
      2007041733

Editor: Christine Florie
Publisher: Michelle Bisson
Art Director: Anahid Hamparian
Series Designer: Virginia Pope

Photo research by Connie Gardner

Rebus images, with the exception of coyote and jackrabbit, provided courtesy of *Dorling Kindersley*.

Cover photo by Gary Meszaros/Dembinsky Photo Associates

The photographs in this book are used by permission and through the courtesy of:
Darrell Gulin/CORBIS, p. 2 (jackrabbit); George H. Huey/CORBIS, p. 3 (coyote); *Animals, Animals*: Sylvilagus auduboni, 5; George H. Huey, 7; Joe McDonald, 19; *Minden Pictures*: Michael and Patricia Fogden, 9; *Getty Images*: Michael Durham, 11; *Digital Railroad*: Heidi and Hans Jurgen Koch, 17; *Art Life Images*: age fotostock, 13; *Corbis*: Lynda Richardson, 15; Karen Hunt, 21.

Printed in Malaysia
1 3 5 6 4 2